THE EXTRAORDINARY BOOK THAT MAKES YOU FEEL HAPPY

Written by Poppy O'Neill

Illustrated by Caribay M. Benavides

Consultant: Wynne Kinder, MEd

TEAR OFF, CUT OUT, and MAKE the PROJECTS. STORE them in your HAPPY POCKET at the back of this BOOK.

EARTHAWARE
KIDS

A Message from Wynne Kinder,
Teacher and mindfulness expert

Hello, Grown-Ups!

Your extraordinary young person will explore, discover, and enjoy this extraordinary book—sometimes solo and other times with your support—through reading, listening, questioning, imagining, cutting, folding, gluing, playing, sharing, and caring.

Happy moments might emerge at the beginning, middle, or end of your child's exploration of this unique experience. For some, the joy will come from curiosity fueled by novelty and newness. For others, it will come while immersed in the hands-on crafts or mindful practices. Still others will find contentment engaging with the final products.

Please encourage the full range of your child's experience and patiently observe their experiences of curiosity, connection, hope, and even a little confusion along the way. As necessary, allow for pauses and put-downs (of the book) as well as possible missteps and mistakes throughout their creative process. And keep in mind that guiding young readers with gentle suggestions and wisely placed sticky notes can be very encouraging.

Enjoy watching your child delve into this engaging, page-turning guide to growing happy.

You know your child best, so for safety, be sure to closely monitor their use of tools such as scissors, movements such as stretches, and personal connections to emotions or memories.

Hey, Extraordinary Reader!

This book is made for you. It fits you. Because just like you, this book is extraordinary—it is **unique, useful,** and **fun** too!

The Extraordinary Book That Makes You Feel Happy is unique because the way you read it and create with it will be different from what everyone else does with their books.

It is **useful** because it can inspire you to notice the real you, help you figure out what you need, and guide you to take really good care of yourself.

And **fun** too? You bet! This book is full of so many fun things to **explore, try, do, play, make, create, share,** and **keep.** There's even a **special pocket** to store your projects and treasures at the back.

Wait! How can both fun and useful be in the same book? They seem so different! Well, just as you can be wild and restful, caring and playful, and silly and calm, your extraordinary book can too.

Here's how to get started

- Sit in a comfortable spot, maybe in your favorite place to settle.
- Shift around until you can be comfortable. Pause there for a bit.
- Take a look at the contents and choose where to start:
    - at the beginning?
        - with a word or phrase that matches how you feel?
            - with perhaps a fun idea that catches your eye?
                - Go there and take your time looking, reading, and imagining.

Remember, you can feel happy by noticing, choosing, trying, learning, caring, and exploring your extraordinary self within the pages of this extraordinary book.

Enjoy!

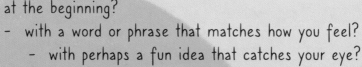

CONTENTS

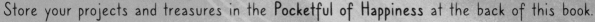

Store your projects and treasures in the **Pocketful of Happiness** at the back of this book.

MOVE YOUR BODY
to ease your emotions

Moving your body helps emotions to move through and out of you. When your body moves, your brain feels good. Let's move!

Practice yoga to stretch your body.

Take a deep breath in and out. Shake and wiggle your whole body in whichever way feels good.

Pigeon pose

Hold your head up high and breathe deeply.

Butterfly pose

Flutter your knees up and down.

Swan pose

Feel the stretch in your legs.

You are the expert on how your body feels.
How does your body want to move right now?

Would it feel good to jump up and down?

Do your arms want to sweep back and forth?

How do your hips want to move?

Use the yoga cards when you need a good stretch. Hold each pose for three breaths.

Bear pose

See how extraight you can get your legs.

Lizard pose

How low can you go?

Gorilla pose

Feel the stretch behind your knees.

TAKE CARE OF YOUR BODY
to take care of your mind

2
Make some delicious, healthy snacks.

Eating healthily, drinking plenty of water, and getting enough sleep are the building blocks of a happy mind.

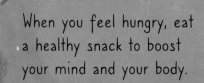

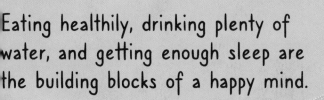

When you feel hungry, eat a healthy snack to boost your mind and your body.

Popsicles

6 oz. yogurt— dairy, coconut, or almond

2 tbsp. natural sweetener— honey, maple, or agave syrup

Fresh, soft fruit

1 Mash your fruit into a puree.

2 Mix in the yogurt and sweetener.

3 Pour into popsicle moulds and freeze for 4 hours.

4 Your popsicles are ready to enjoy!

When it's time to sleep, imagine starlight shining on your toes, relaxing them one by one.

As the light moves up your body, think about relaxing each part of you.

When the starlight reaches the top of your head, you're ready for sleep.

Energy balls

8 oz. chopped dates

2 oz. oats

1 tbsp. maple syrup

optional extras—cocoa powder, chopped nuts, desiccated coconut

1 Soak the dates in hot water for five minutes.

2 Drain the dates and mix all ingredients together.

3 Squish into 1 in. balls.

4 Chill in the fridge for at least half an hour.

30"

SPEAK YOUR MIND
because your voice matters

Speaking about your thoughts, feelings, and experiences helps you to understand yourself and lets others get to know the real you.

I LIKE

I NEED

WHY?

WHAT IF?

Sometimes we keep our thoughts and feelings inside, but what's important needs to be let out.

GUESS WHAT!

LOOK AT ME!

I THINK

CAN I?

I FEEL

I DON'T LIKE

Use this journal to write about your thoughts and feelings every day for a week.

My Journal

Tuesday

Today I liked...

_____
_____
_____
_____

Thursday

Today I felt...

_____
_____
_____
_____

Saturday

Today was tricky because...

_____
_____
_____
_____

Even if a problem can't be solved, talking to someone you trust will help you feel better.

WHY?

GUESS WHAT?

WHAT IF?

I NEED

I THINK

I FEEL

I LIKE

CAN I?

Thread your journal pages together with string.

Monday	Wednesday	Friday	Sunday
Today I went...	Today I enjoyed...	Today I felt...	Today I learned...

TAKE A DEEP BREATH
to relax your mind and body

4

Make a starry breathing wand.

Imagine breathing in the Solar System.

Taking a big breath wakes you up and gets you ready for anything.

Breathing out is one of the simplest ways to create calm.

Stretch up high and fill with air.

Breathe out slowly and reach down gradually to catch a shooting star.

TURN OVER to find out how to make this starry strip into your very own breathing wand.

If you feel anxious, take a finger hike. It will make you feel much calmer. Walk your finger up and down the mountains as you breathe in and out to the count of five.

Breathe in as you walk your finger up the mountain.

Breathe out as you run your finger down the other side.

Count slowly each time— 1-2-3-4-5.

You can also take a hike up and down your fingers, breathing in and out as you go.

Make a breathing wand

You will need

recycled card (8 in. x 3 in.)

tissue paper

tape

scissors

1 Cut out a card strip or use the other side of this page. Roll into a cylinder and fix with tape.

2 Cut the tissue paper into strips about ½ in. x 8 in. and tape the strips inside one edge.

3 Take a big breath in and watch the streamers wave as you breathe ou

RESET
to rest and relax

Sometimes you need to reset before you can rest and relax. You can let go of extra energy in lots of different ways.

Try running, jumping, skipping, or Hula-Hooping.

To rest and relax, cut out the mosaic squares below to make a soothing piece of art.

Relax with art

Find an old magazine and
cut out lots of little squares
in different colors. Match the
colors to this picture
and stick them on.

Make mosaic a

Create your own
pictures by cutting out,
arranging, and gluing the
little squares below.

BE POSITIVE
—believe in yourself and try your best

When you're learning something new, each mistake helps you improve. When you think you can't do something, try adding "yet."

I can't do any tricks on my skateboard...

...yet.

Each time you practice, you make progress.

You can do it!

Just be you.

You are braver than you think!

Try your best.

Keep going!

Reach for the stars.

One step at a time.

Be curious.

When you look for positivity, you'll find it all around you.

respect

love

strength

courage

kindness

joy

care

peace

hope

resilience

Stick these positive messages up in your room to keep you motivated, or give them to a friend.

Imagine the possibilities!

You've got this.

You can take a break.

You are determined.

You are enough.

You are awesome!

You are kind.

You have courage.

CARE FOR YOUR BODY
because it's your forever home

Your body is incredible in so many ways. When you are kind to your body, you feel good all over.

My lungs help me take a deep breath.

My body helps me explore the world.

My feet can dance.

I can hear my heart beating.

My muscles keep me moving.

Wriggle your toes.

Stretch your arms.

Run your fingers through your hair.

Sit comfortably and say thank you to your body!

Thank you eyes for showing me the world.

Thank you tongue for the delicious tastes.

Thank you legs for helping me to walk and play.

How will you say thank you to your body?

Pick a card whenever you want to show love to your body.

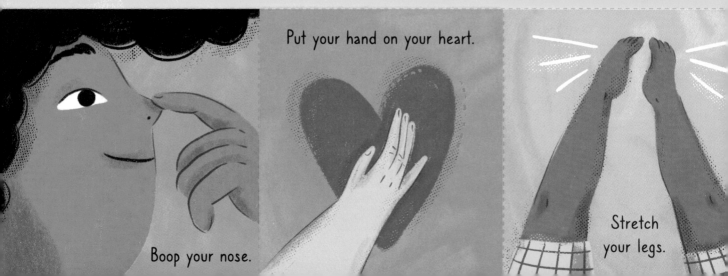

Boop your nose.

Put your hand on your heart.

Stretch your legs.

GUIDE YOUR THOUGHTS
to calm them

Sometimes thoughts can spin out of control. Learn to guide them by visiting a secret garden in your mind.

Picture a magical garden. What can you see? You can fill it with anything you like.

Cut out and arrange these cards. You can lay them next to each other in any order to help you imagine your secret garden.

Calm your mind

Focus on your finger as you follow the moonlit trail through this garden maze.

BE TRUE TO YOURSELF
because it's wonderful to be you

What inspires you?

What do you love to do?

What makes you different is what makes you special. Your interests are a big part of what makes you unique.

What do you know lots about?

Write to three people who are special to you.

To:

To:

To:

Be yourself and shine your light.
If we were all the same, the world
would be a very boring place!

When you let your true self
shine, true friends will find you.

You're special because

From:

You're special because

From:

You're special because

From:

BE MINDFUL
—take a moment to just "be"

Your senses and imagination can help you practice just being.

Close your eyes and picture the ocean.

As you breathe in, imagine the waves moving forward.

As you breathe out, think about the waves moving away.

Take a deep breath for a really big wave.

Color in the waves. Watch as color fills the gaps.

Close your eyes and imagine a beautiful forest all around you. In front of you is a pond of still water.

You can see your reflection in the pond. You can see the trees and sky in it too.

Swirl your finger around in the water and watch the ripples it makes.

When the water is still again, open your eyes.

Color this pond like the one you imagined.

RESPECT YOURSELF
and be your own best friend

Treat yourself the way you would like be treated. Be kind to yourself and be your own biggest fan.

I WILL FEEL PROUD

I WILL STAND UP FOR MYSELF

I WILL BE A GOOD FRIEND

I WILL TRY MY BEST

I WILL BE BRAVE

Each morning, think of one wish for the day.

Say kind words to yourself. The more you say them, the more you will believe they are true.

I AM BRAVE

I AM KIND

My happiness is important

MY FEELINGS MATTER

My mind is positive

ad string gh the holes ake bunting.

FIND HAPPINESS
to grow happiness

12
Send some happiness on a postcard.

The more time you spend doing things that bring you happiness, the easier it becomes to look for happiness everywhere you go.

Smiling works like magic. It makes your mind and body feel relaxed and happy.

Sharing happiness helps to grow happiness. Make someone smile by sending them a postcard.

Fill a shelf, box, or drawer with things that make you smile.

Visit your special place whenever you need a boost of happiness.

NAME YOUR EMOTIONS
to accept them all

Naming your feelings can help you learn what's really going on inside. There's no such thing as a bad or a wrong emotion.

What do you feel today?

confident

happy

surprised

scared

angry

sad

✂ Cut out and arrange the features to make different faces.

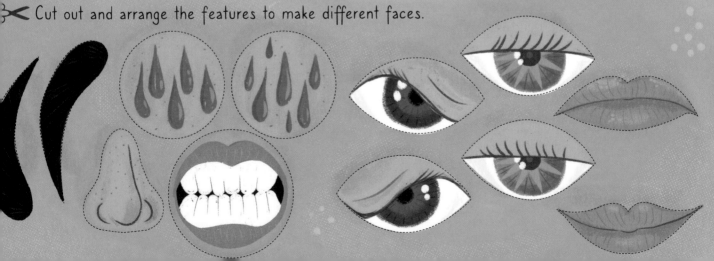

Emotions are like colors. The rainbow is not complete without all of them.

Everyone feels a whole rainbow of emotions, even if they don't always show every color!

The emotions you feel are part of what makes you special.

EXPRESS YOURSELF
to let your feelings out

When you let your feelings show, you are being true to you. Your emotions can tell a truthful story.

I could fly away!

I feel warm inside.

I'm in a spin.

I feel like dancing.

There's a fierce dragon inside me.

I feel gloomy.

I'm curious.

Which words and pictures could you use to express your feelings?

Make a spinning dancer

1 Cut out the pieces.

2 Thread a rubber band through each hole.

3 Fasten each rubber band by threading it back through itself.

Big feelings can be tricky to show on the outside.
Dancing lets you express yourself freely.

Put some music on and dance!

Twist the rubber
bands and let the
circle spin.

What do
you see?

FIND GRATITUDE
in the little things

Practice looking for things to be grateful for. You'll be able to find joy in the most unexpected places.

Look around you. How many things can you spot that you feel gratitude for?

Choose two people to give these cards to and write why you are thankful.

Thank you

Thank you

Who are you grateful for?

Dear ....

Thank you for
....
....
....
....

from ....

Dear ....

Thank you for
....
....
....
....

from ....

LOVE YOURSELF
because you are unique

You are always with yourself, so make sure you are a good friend to you.

Care for yourself by giving yourself a big hug.

Make a self-love scrapbook all about you. You can draw on the pages, or stick things on with glue.

I'm proud of...

....

....

....

This is me

A leaf from my favorite place

My favorite recipe

Find your anchor

Emotions are like the sea, always moving and changing.
Create an anchor of positive thoughts to steady you,
however many waves might come.

I love myself.

I am safe.

I can try my best.

It's OK to make mistak

My feelings matter.

I am good.

I am kind.

Thinking and saying positive words to yourself helps you feel
calm and be kind to yourself no matter what is happening.

My favorite thing

My three wishes

1
2
3

My best hug

I'm grateful for...

TELL YOUR STORY
to own it

Your story is unique and you are the one who gets to tell it. Celebrate your story and feel proud of who you are!

What are you proud of?

Who gave you your name? Does it have meaning?

What is your favorite thing to do with your family?

What do you want your life to be like when you grow up?

Do you know any stories about your family?

Stick or draw your favorite "you" pictures into the frames below.

Baby Me

School Me

Birthday Me

Cool Me

Your family is part of your story. Families are all different—they don't always look how you'd expect. Can you add photos or drawings of your family to the tree?

Who do you live with?

Who is youngest?

Who is oldest in your family?

What other children are in your family?

Who in your family lives close by?

Who in your family lives far away?

Stick pictures of your family into the frames below.
Fold along the dotted lines to make a zigzag display.

FACE YOUR FEARS
to see that you are stronger than them

Fears tell us so much. Which ones can we work through and let go of?

The mouse looks huge—that's really scary!

Sometimes we get scared, even when we're not in danger.

But look—now we can see the mouse is small and cute.

Make paper airplanes to fly your fears away

1 Find a rectangular piece of paper and write your fears and worries on it.

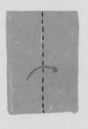

2 Fold the paper in half lengthways.

3 Open it out again and fold two corners in to meet in the middle.

4 Fold the edges again to meet in the middle.

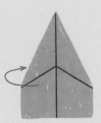

5 Fold your airplane in half so that the flaps are on the outside.

KEEP YOUR COOL
to handle those big emotions

Learning how to calm your feelings takes practice. Big emotions are like clouds—they pass across the sky. You can watch them go. They don't stick around very long.

Anger can feel like a storm inside you.

Sadness might feel like a gray, rainy day.

Fear can make you freeze like snow.

But feelings pass. Before you know it, you'll feel sunny again.

Moving your body can help stormy emotions feel calm again. Try these things.

Run,

skip,

dance,

jump,

or bounce.

1 – 2 – 3 – 4 – 5 – 6 – 7 – 8 – 9 – 10

Count to ten slowly.

Make a calming fidget spinner

1 ✂ Cut out the circles below. Push a coin into the slot.

2 Spin to see the calming patterns.

FIND TIME TO BE ALONE
—you'll be in good company

When you feel good hanging out with yourself, you can create happiness anywhere, anytime.

Have fun exploring your limitless imagination.

Complete the pages to imagine Patch's great adventure. Thread them together with string.

Patch's Great Adventure

Written and illustrated
by _____

1

3

5

Luckily...

7

When you're by yourself, you can go at your own pace. What will you find?

Magical things happen when you spend time alone. What will you discover

Once upon a time, there was a brave little dog called Patch.

Suddenly, Patch saw a...

But then...

2

4

6

8

CHOOSE ANOTHER STORY
to see a different point of view

There is often more than one way to see things. Look carefully. What do you see? Turn the book upside down to see the answer.

Do you see rabbits, or ducks? They are both there.

Cut out the pieces to make your glasses. Fold along the dotted lines and glue the arms to the back of the frames.

glue here

glue here

There's always more than one way to look at things.
Try to find a positive story.

A long journey
can be boring...

...or the chance to imagine
a perfect adventure!

fold here

glue here

glue here

Put on these glasses
when you need to remind
yourself to look at things
in a different way.

What do you see?

BUILD PATIENCE
—it's worth the wait

22

Save your sunflower seeds to make seedy, cheesy bread sticks.

flower

bud

leaves

shoot

Plant a tiny sunflower seed in the ground. Be patient.

2 weeks

4 weeks

8 weeks

12 weeks

seeds

When you feel OK about waiting, life gets a lot less frustrating. Practice being patient by growing a sunflower.

16 weeks

After 16 weeks, you can collect the seeds to eat!

Bake seedy, cheesy breadsticks

Ingredients

| 1 c. bread flour | 1 oz. cheddar cheese | ½ c. warm water | 1 tsp. salt | 1 tsp. oil | 1 tbsp. sunflower seeds | 1 tbsp. yeast |

Equipment

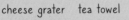
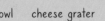

parchment paper

wooden spoon

patience!

bowl   cheese grater   tea towel   baking tray

1 Put all the ingredients into a bowl. Mix everything together until you have a ball of dough.

2 Cover the bowl with a damp tea towel. Leave in a warm place for an hour. Wait patiently.

There are all sorts of ways to practice being patient.

When it's raining outside...

...build a domino run inside.

When it's dry outdoors...

...collect and arrange colored leaves in a pattern.

3 After one hour, remove the tea towel. How much has your dough risen?

4 Tear the dough into six pieces. Roll and squash them into sausage shapes.

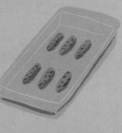

5 Put your seedy breadsticks onto a baking tray.

6 Ask an adult to help you bake them for 20 minutes or until golden brown.

Enjoy your seedy, cheesy breadsticks. They were worth the wait!

IMAGINE
to explore your creativity

When you use your imagination, anything is possible.

23
Create and decorate an amazing mask.

Cut out the mask and use your imagination to decorate it.

Welcome to the masquerade ball!
What will you dress up as?

You can decorate
your mask with
almost anything—
fabric, paper,
crayons, paints,
craft materials,
nature finds...

SPEND TIME IN NATURE
to find your happy place

Being outdoors is good for you in so many ways. All your senses work to make you feel happier. Step outside and explore your garden, park, or nearby woodland.

What can you hear?

What can you smell?

What can you see?

Go barefoot to let the grass tickle your feet.

Get closer to nature

Climb a tree.

Make bark rubbings.

Build a den.

Go on a nature scavenger hunt

Cut out the pictures below and take them with you outdoors.

When you spot something, put the picture in a jar. What did you see?

EASE INTO CHANGE
—things can work out

Changes can feel scary and exciting at the same time.

egg

butterfly

caterpillar

chrysalis

A butterfly changes many times in its life span.

Some changes can be really hard. When you miss someone, talking about your feelings helps your heart feel happier.

✂ Cut out the hearts. When you're away from someone special, give them one half and keep the other, so you can still feel close.

CREATE
to set your imagination free

When you create something unique, your mind feels happy, calm, and free. Use pens and pencils to draw a fantastic place from your imagination.

What adventures could happen?

What would happen if the characters below visited your imagined place?

fold here   fold here   fold here   fold here   fold here

Create your own miniature film set in a shoebox.
Use recycled and craft materials to decorate the box
and to make furniture, props, and sets.

What kind of building
will you create?

Cut out the characters below
or make your own. Now you're
ready to direct your first film!

fold here   fold here   fold here   fold here   fold here

REACH OUT
to share happiness

Being around other people—especially the ones who love and accept you—builds happiness. Who makes you feel happy?

How to play dragons and ladders

Choose a counter each. Decide who will go first.

Spin the spinner and move your counter the number of steps the spinner lands on.

turn over...

✂

Cut out all the counters and the spinner. Stick a pencil through the hole in the spinner, pointy end down.

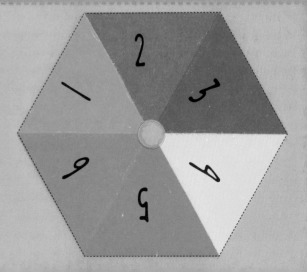

2 3 4 5 6 1

If you land on a ladder, climb up it.

If you land on a dragon, slide down it.

The winner is the first to reach the 100 square.

HUG

to hold each other close

A hug helps calm your emotions and makes you feel good.

Try a handshake, fist bump, elbow tap, wave, or wink, too!

If there is someone you can't hug in person, send a paper hug.

✂ Cut out this hug.
Write a lovely message to someone special.

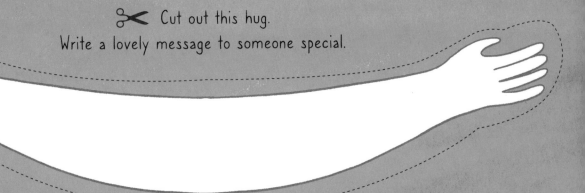

Being close to a tree makes you feel calm. Find a tree and hug it close.

The tree is alive, like you. Can you feel it growing?

Use snail mail to post your hug.

BE GENEROUS
to spread happiness

You are special and your kindness can make the world a brighter place.

29
Make a window picture for your neighbors.

YOU MATTER

ALWAYS BE YOU

SHINE BRIGHT

Paint a picture or message on a pebble and leave it to be found.

Cut out this template to make a window picture.

Passersby will love seeing your picture lit up.

Make a window picture

1 Carefully cut out the row of houses and pop out their windows.

2 Stick strips of colorful tissue paper over the windows.

3 Hang your masterpiece in your window.

SHOW UNDERSTANDING
by imagining how others feel

excited

proud

happy

energetic

When it is hard to understand people and what they do, try to see life from their view. Imagine you could live their life, walk in their shoes.

sad

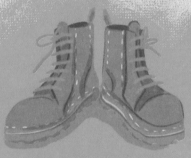

angry

relaxed

tired

lay feelings
harades

ll you need is
ome friends
nd a scarf.

HAPPY

ANGRY

WORRIED

PROUD

Showing you care can be enough to make someone feel better.

I'M GLAD YOU'RE HERE

THAT MAKES SENSE

ARE YOU OK?

TELL ME MORE

I'M LISTENING

HOW CAN I HELP?

I'M HERE FOR YOU

When someone's fee[l] down, kind words are like a big umbrella o[n] a rainy day.

EXCITED

SURPRISED

SAD

AFRAID

How to play

✂ 1 Cut out the feelings cards and shuffle them.

2 Pick a card each. Without looking at the card, put it on your forehead, facing out, with a scarf holding it in place.

3 Take turns to ask questions to help guess your card, be careful not to name any feeling in your questions

4 Keep going until everyone has corr[ectly] guessed their card[.]